MONARCHS & THE MUSE

MONARCHS & the MUSE

Poems by Monarchs
and Princes of England,
Scotland and Wales

introduced by
C. V. Wedgwood

edited by
Sally Purcell

illustrated by
Priscilla Eckhard

Fyfield Books
A CARCANET PRESS PUBLICATION

We are grateful to Macmillan (London and Basingstoke) for
permission to publish Joseph P. Clancy's translations from the Welsh

SBN 85635 033 8

First published 1972
by Carcanet Press
Pin Farm, South Hinksey
Oxford

Printed in Great Britain
by W & J Mackay Limited, Chatham

For Elizabeth Jennings

Contents

Illustrator's Note

THE designs for the decorations are taken from the personal crests, badges and supporters of the monarchs, except in the cases of Alfred and Canute, whose symbols are based on Viking and Anglo-Saxon motifs.

I am indebted to Charles Boutell's *English Heraldry* (London, 1889) for the relevant information.

PRISCILLA ECKHARD

Introduction

How many kings and princes in the British Isles wrote poetry? Not very many, one would have thought, but this anthology reveals a surprising number of monarchs who aspired to be poets and quite a few who really were poets.

Here are poems ranging over a thousand years, from those of Alfred the Great, who combined a considerable gift for literature with an even greater gift for government, to a contribution from George IV who, to be frank, scores no higher marks as a poet than he does as a King. Still, he must be given credit for trying, and his verses to Lady Sarah Campbell, written in 1781 when he was an impressionable boy of 20, have a pleasing youthfulness and an elegant competence.

There are some surprises. Who would have guessed, from his dim reputation in the history books, that 'poor Fred', the unloved son of George II and father of George III, had it in him to compose poems—well, verses anyway—in both French and English? One begins to speculate on the possibility of a sensitive spirit stifled by the tedium of the Hanoverian court and poisoned by the spitefulness of his family. Poor Fred indeed. . . .

The Scottish Kings have perhaps the highest score for real poetry. James I leads the field with his exquisite 'Kingis Quhair', well represented here with a helpful glossary for the general reader. Then there is the enigmatic, brilliant James V—a poetic temperament if ever there was one—and the careful but by no means insensitive work of the scholarly James VI. His mother, Mary Queen of Scots, is represented by poems in both French and English, and even his father, the deplorable Darnley, versified some sage advice on the conduct of princes which he never thought of putting into practice himself.

Two Welsh princes indicate something of the poetic riches of the mediaeval Welsh tradition, and poems of Richard Coeur de Lion translated from the Provençal, beautiful in themselves, also remind us of the breadth and richness of the linguistic sources from which English literature derives.

Indeed it is an additional merit of this discriminating and varied anthology that it offers so many clues to the historic imagination, so many subjects for deeper thought. In the ninth century King Alfred translated the *Consolations of Philosophy* of Boethius, and seven hundred years later Queen Elizabeth I also tried her hand at it. Each translation filters the fifth century Latin through a different type of verbal pattern and a different way of thought. But both bear witness to the immense and continuous popularity enjoyed from early mediaeval times to the late Renaissance by the dignified Christian stoicism of a late Roman statesman writing in a barbarian world. When did Boethius cease to be familiar to all educated and thoughtful men?

Miss Purcell has gathered from some of the least frequented by-ways of history and from many different literary sources an anthology full of interest and delight.

C. V. WEDGWOOD

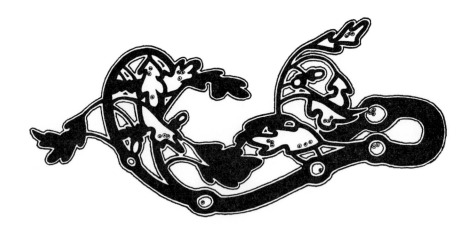

ALFRED

King of Wessex. Born at Wantage in 849. Succeeded to the throne in 871 and spent the rest of his reign campaigning against the Danes who were overrunning the country. Translated Bede's and Orosius' histories and St. Gregory's *Pastoral Care* into Anglo-Saxon. The Boethius was probably begun about 887. Died in 901 and was buried at Winchester.

King Alfred's version of Boethius' 'Cum polo Phoebus'

Tha se Wisdom eft wordhord onleac,
sang sothcwidas, and thus selfa cwaeth:
thonne sio sunne sweotolost scineth,
hadrost of hefone, hraethe bioth athistrod
ealle ofir eorthen othre steorran;
forthaem hiora birhtu ne bith auht
to gesettane with thaere sunnan leoht.
thonne smolte blaewth suthan and westan
wind under wolcnum, thonne weaxath hrathe
feldes blostman, faegen thaet hi moton.
ac se stearca storm thonne he strong cymth,
northan and eastan, he genimeth hrathe
thaere rosan wlite; and eac tha ruman sae
northerne yst nede gebaedeth
thaet hio strange geondstyred on stathu beateth.
Eala thaet on eorthan auht faestlices
weorces on worulde ne wunath aefre.

Then Wisdom again unlocked his treasure of words, sang truths and spoke thus: When the sun shines clearest and brightest in heaven, quickly all the other stars (that shine) over the earth are darkened. Their brightness is nothing beside the sun's light. When south and west wind blow mildly under the clouds, the flowers of the field soon grow, glad that they may. But the violent storm, when it comes in strength from north and east, quickly takes the rose's brightness. And the northern tempest, strongly forced by necessity, beats and hurls the broad sea against the shores. Alas, that in this world no lasting work ever remains!

Aeala, thu scippend scirra tungla,
hefones and eorthan; thu on heah-setle
ecum ricsast, and thu ealne hraethe
hefon ymbhwearfest, and thurh thine halige miht
tunglu genedest thaet hi the to herath.
swylce seo sunne sweartra nihta
thiostro adwaesceth, thurh thine meht,
blacum leohte, beorhte steorran
mona gemetgath; thurh thinra meahta sped
hwilum eac tha sunnan sines bereafath
beorhtan leohtes, thonne hit gebyrigan maeg
thaet swa geneahsne nede weorthath.
swelce thone maeran morgensteorran
the we othre namen oefensteorra
nemnan herath, thu genedest thone
thaet he thaere sunnan sith bewitige.
geara gehwelce he gongan sceal,
beforan feran. hwaet thu, faeder, wercest
sumurlange dagas swithe hate;

O creator of the bright stars, of heaven and earth, ruling forever on your high throne, swiftly you turn the whole heaven round and by your holy power make the stars obey. Thus the sun drives away the black nights' darkness, through your power, the moon dims bright stars with her pale light; by your power she sometimes deprives the sun of his light, when she happens to be so near. Also the splendid morning-star, that we also hear called the evening-star, you compel to keep to the sun's path: every year he shall move on before it. O Father, you make the long summer days very hot; you have allotted

3

thaem winterdagum wundrum sceorta
tida getiohhast. thu thaem treowum selest
suthan and westan, tha aer se swearta storm
northan and eastan benumen haefde
leafa gehwelces thurh thone lathran wind.
eala hwaet, on eorthan ealla gesceafta
hyrath thinre haese; doth on heofonum swa some
mode und maegne, butan men anum,
se with thinum willan wyrceth oftost.
wella, thu eca and thu aelmihtiga,
ealra gesceafta sceppend and reccend,
ara thinum earmum eorthan tudre,
monna cynne, thurh thinra mehta sped.
hwi thu ece God aefre wolde
thaet sio wyrd on gewill wendan sceolde
yflum monnan aelles swa swithe?
hio ful oft dereth unscyldegum.
sittath yfele men giond eorthricu
on heahsetlum, halige thriccath
under heora fotum. firum uncuth
hwi sio wyrd swa wó wendan sceolde
swa sint gehydde her on worulde
geond burga fela beorhte craeftas.

wonderfully short time to winter days. You give south and west winds for the trees which earlier the black storms of north and east with a more hateful wind had stripped of every leaf. On earth all creatures obey your command, and they do the same in heaven, with will and power, except man alone, who most often works against your will. O eternal, almighty one, maker and ruler of all creatures, spare your wretched earthly offspring, mankind, by your power. Why, eternal God, should you ever intend that Fate should so favour evil men? Very often he harms the innocent. Wicked men sit on high thrones in earthly kingdoms, treading the holy underfoot. Men do not know why fate should turn out so wrongly. Thus in this world, in many cities, bright virtues are hidden.

unrihtwise eallum tidum
habbath on hospe tha the him sindon
rihtes wisran, rices wyrthran.
bith thaet lease lot lange hwile
bewrigen mid wrencum. nu on worulde her
monnum ne deriath máne athas.
gif thu nu, waldend, ne wilt wirde steoran,
ac on selfwille sigan laetest,
thonne ic wat thaet te wile woruldmen tweogan
geond foldan sceat, buton fea ane.
eala, min Dryhten, thu the ealle ofersihst
worulde gesceafta, wlit nu on moncyn
mildum eagum, nu hi on monegum her
worulde ythum wynnath and swincath
earme eorthwaran; ara him nu tha.

    Wicked men always despise those who are wiser in righteousness, worthier to rule. False craftiness is long hidden by deceits. Now here in this world harm no man, make no false oaths. Ruler, if you will not now control Fortune, but let her rush on unchecked in her own way, I know that many men throughout the world, all but a few, will begin to doubt. O my Lord, over-seer of all the world's creatures, look now on mankind with gentle eyes, now that they strive and struggle in the waves of this world; spare the poor dwellers on earth now.

Extract from King Alfred's version of Boethius' 'Quicumque solam'

Theah hwa aethele sie eorldge byrdu,
welum geweorthad, and on wlencum thio
duguthum diore, death thaes ne scrifeth
thonne him rum forlaet rodora waldend;
ac he thone welegan waedlum gelice
efnmaerne gedeth aelces thinges.
hwaer sint nu thaes wisan Welandes ban
thaes goldsmithes, the waes geo maerost?
forthy ic cwaeth thaes wisan Welandes ban
forthy aengum ne maeg eorthbuendra
se craeft losian the him Crist onlaenth.
ne maeg mon aefre thy eth aenne wraeccan
his craeftes beniman, the mon oncearran maeg
sunnan onswifan, and thisne swiftan rodor
of his rihtryne rinca aenig.
hwa wat nu thaes wisan Welandes ban,
on hwelcum hi hlaewa hrusan theccen?
hwaer is nu se rica Romana wita
and se aroda the we ymb sprecath,
hiora heretoga, se gehaten waes
mid thaem burgwarum, Brutus nemned?
hwaer is eac se wisa and se weorthgeorna
and se faestraeda folces hyrde
se waes uthwita aelces thinges
cene and craeftig, thaem waes Caton nama?
hi waeron gefyrn forthgewitene
nat naenig mon hwaer hi nu sindon.

If any be noble, born an earl, abounding in wealth and magnificent in riches, Death cares nothing for him, once heaven's ruler has given him a free hand; he makes the rich like the poor, equally famous in everything. Where are now wise Wayland's bones, once the most famous of goldsmiths? I said wise Wayland's bones, because no earthly man's skill perishes that Christ has granted him, nor may anyone deprive a poor man of his craft, any more than he can turn back the sun and the swift turning sky from its right course. Who knows now under what heap of earth lie hidden wise Wayland's bones? Where is now the powerful councillor of the Romans, the bold man we speak of, their consul the citizens called Brutus? Where is now the wise, ambitious, steadfast guardian of the people, a philosopher in all things, keen and skilful, that was named Cato? They departed long ago; no man knows where they are now.

6

CANUTE

Born in about 994, son of Sweyn, King of Denmark. Invaded England and in 1013 dethroned Ethelred the Unready. Succeeded his father in 1014 as King of the English and Danes, and claimed the Norwegian crown by marriage. Died in 1035 and was succeeded by his son Hardicanute as King of England.

Excerpt from the twelfth-century chronicle Liber *Eliensis* (ed. D. J. Stewart, 1848). The King, while on a journey by water to Ely, heard the chanting of the monks (*clare divinas horas modulantes*), and at once

'ipsemet ore proprio jocunditatem cordis exprimens, cantilenam his verbis Anglice composuit, dicens, cujus exordium sic continetur:

> Merie sungen the Muneches binnen Ely.
> Tha Cnut ching reu ther by.
> Roweth cnites noer the land.
> and here we thes Muneches saeng.

"Dulce cantaverunt monachi in Ely, dum Canutus rex navigaret prope ibi, nunc milites navigate propius ad terram, et simul audiamus monachorum harmoniam," *et caetera quae sequuntur, quae usque hodie in choris publice cantantur et in proverbiis memorantur.'*

With his own mouth expressing the joy he felt in his heart, he composed a song in English, in these words, which begins thus: 'Merrily sang the monks of Ely, as Canute the King rowed by; row, knights, nearer to the land, and let us hear these monks' song', and the rest that follows, which to this day is sung at dances among the people and remembered in popular sayings.

8

RICHARD I

Born at Beaumont Palace in Oxford in 1157. Became Count of Poitou in right of his mother, and King of England in 1189. On his return from the Third Crusade, he was shipwrecked and imprisoned by the German Emperor. The story of his rescue by the faithful minstrel Blondel is unlikely to be true. After the payment of a vast ransom, he was brought back to England and crowned at Winchester. Died of a wound received from a crossbow while besieging the castle of Chalus in the Limousin, in 1199, and was succeeded by his brother John.

Poem written from prison in autumn or early winter of 1193, addressed to his half-sister Marie de Champagne. I give here the Provençal version, with the extra verses 5 and 6 from the Old French version.

Ja nuls hom pres non dira sa razon
Adrechament, si com hom dolens non;
Mas per conort deu hom faire canson:
Pro n'ay d'amis, mas paure son li don,
Ancta lur es, si per ma rezenson
Soi sai dos yvers pres.

Or sapchon ben miey hom e miey baron,
Angles, Norman, Peytavin e Gascon,
Qu'ieu non ay ja si paure compagnon
Qu'ieu laissasse, per aver, en preison;
Non ho dic mia per nulla retraison,
Mas anquar soi ie pres.

Car sai eu ben per ver, certanament,
Qu'hom mort ni pres n'a amic ni parent,
E si.m laissan per aur ni per argent,
Mal m'es per mi, mas pieg m'es per ma gent,
Qu'apres ma mort n'auran reprochament,
Si sai mi laisson pres.

No.m meravilh s'ieu ay lo cor dolent,
Que mos senher met ma terra en turment;
No li membra del nostre sagrament
Que nos feimes el Sans cominalment;
Ben sai de ver que gaire longament
Non serai en sai pres.

(Ce sevent bien Angevin et Torain,
Cil bacheler qui or sont riche et sain,
Qu'encombrez sui loing d'els en altrui mains!
Forment m'amoient, mais or ne m'aiment grain;
De beles armes sont ores vuit li plain,
Por tant que je sui pres.

Mes compaignons cui j'amoie et cui j'ain,
Cels de Cahiu et cels de Porcherain,
Me di, chançon, qu'il ne sont pas certain;
Qu'onques vers els n'oi le cuer fals ne vain,
S'il me guerroient, il font molt que vilain
Tant com je serai pres.)

Suer comtessa, vostre pretz sobeiran
Sal Dieus, e gard la bella qu'ieu am tan,
Ni per cui soi ja pres.

    No man in prison can express his mind so skilfully as one who is free from distress; but for comfort's sake he may make a song. I have many friends, but poor are their gifts, and it is to their shame if I must lie in prison two winters for want of ransom. My vassals and my men, English, Normans, Poitevins and Gascons, know well that I have no companion so poor that I would let him remain in prison for want of ransom; I do not speak this in reproach, yet I still lie in prison. For I know well it is the truth that a dead or imprisoned man has no friends nor relatives; and if they leave me here for gold or silver, it grieves me for myself, but more so for my people, for the shame will be theirs after my death, if they leave me thus in prison. I am not surprised that my heart is sore, while my overlord (Philip of France) torments my land; he has forgotten our oath that we swore together upon holy relics (?), for if he had not I know full well that I should not be left here in prison long. The men of Anjou and Touraine know this well, knights that are happy in fortune and health now, that I am hindered far from them in enemy hands. They used to love me greatly, now they love me not a bit; the fields are all empty of fine arms these days, now that I am imprisoned. My companions whom I loved and still do love, men of Cahors (?) and of the Perche (?)—tell them from me, my song, that they are fickle. My heart was never false or deceitful towards them, and if they make war on me while I am in prison, they treat me very ill. Sister countess, may God guard your sovereign worth, and keep the lady I love so dear, for whom I am in prison here.

By a treaty with Philip Augustus, Richard had exchanged the lordship of the Auvergne for that of Quercy; this displeased the Auvergnat barons, who had thus acquired a much nearer and less sympathetic feudal overlord, the King of France. Richard encouraged them to revolt, promising them assistance, but when, having defied the French King, Gui d'Auvergne went to ask Richard for the promised help, the latter coolly replied that he could not help them against his good friend King Philip, and they were forced to make peace and to render up to Philip their castle of Ussoire. Some time later, in 1195–6, Richard, finding himself at war again with the French King, demanded help from the d'Auvergne brothers, and on their very naturally refusing sent them this *sirventés*.

Dalfin, je.us voill deresnier,
Vos e le conte Guion,
Que an en ceste seison
Vos feïstes bon guerrier,
E vos jurastes ou moi
E m'en portastes liel foi
Com n'Aengris a Rainart,
E sembles dou poil liart.

Vos me laïstes aidier
Por treime de guierdon,
E car savies qu'a Chinon
Non a argent ni denier
E vos voletz riche roi,
Bon d'armes qui vos port foi,
E je suis chiche, coart,
Si.us viretz de l'autre part.

Encore vos voill demandier
D'Ussoire s'il vos siet bon,
Ni si.n prendretz venjeison
Ni logaretz soudadier.
Mas une rien vos outroi,
Si be.us faussastes la loi,
Bon guerrier a l'estandart
Trovaretz le roi Richart.

Je vos vi au comensier
Large de grant messïon;
Mais puis trovetz ochoison
Que por fortz castels levier
Laissastes don e donoi,
E cortz e segre tornoi.
Mais nos cal avoir regart
Que Franssois son Longobart.

Vai sirventés, je t'envoi
En Auvergne, e di moi
As deus comtes de ma part
S'ui mes font pes, Dieu les gart.

Que chaut si garz ment sa foi?
Q'escuiers n'a point de loi;
Mais des or avan se gart
Que n'ait en peior sa part.

    Dalfin, I have a bone to pick with you, you and Count Gui, who have made yourselves such great warriors now; you swore an oath to me, and kept loyal faith to me—as Isengrim did to Reynard; and you certainly resemble that old grey wolf (literally, 'seem greyish of hide'). You stopped helping me at the mere sight of a reward (?), and because you know that in my castle of Chinon there is neither money nor coin—and you want a rich king, strong in arms, who will keep faith with you; and I am mean and cowardly, so you join the other side. Still, I should like to ask you how you are enjoying Ussoire, whether you will be hiring soldiers and taking vengeance. One thing I can assure you, although you have broken faith: you will find King Richard a good warrior by his battle ensign. At first I saw you rich and generous, but then you found the excuse, that fortresses needed building, to abandon generosity and fine manners and courtly life and following tournaments—but it's not for you to care that the French are such skinflints.
    Go, sirventés, I send you to Auvergne, and tell the two Counts from me, if later they make peace, God help them.
    Who cares if a peasant breaks his word? A serving-boy can have no conception of honour. But let him take care from now on that he has not chosen the worse side.

HENRY VI

Became King at the unfortunate age of nine months, on the death of his father Henry V, in 1422. During his reign the Hundred Years' War turned against the English, who lost most of their French possessions; the peasants revolted under Jack Cade; and the Wars of the Roses began, leading to Henry's deposition, imprisonment in the Tower, and probably violent death in 1471. A gentle, mild, ineffectual and deeply religious man, who seems to have suffered from recurrent fits of lethargy and madness, inherited from his grandfather, the mad King Charles VI of France. Henry was the last Lancastrian King, his only son having been killed at the Battle of Tewkesbury in 1471. Founded Eton and King's College, Cambridge.

Poem said to have been written in the Tower, between 1464–9

Kingdoms are but cares,
State is devoid of stay,
Riches are ready snares,
And hasten to decay.

Pleasure is a privy prick,
Which vice doth still provoke;
Pomp, imprompt; and fame, a flame;
Power, a smouldering smoke.

Who meaneth to remove the rock
Out of the slimy mud
Shall mire himself, and hardly 'scape
The swelling of the flood.

HENRY VIII

Born in 1491, second son of Henry VII and Elizabeth of York. A fine singer, composer, sportsman, and scholar in his youth. Became heir to the throne on the death of his elder brother, Prince Arthur, whose widow, Catherine of Aragon, he married. His quarrels with the Church led to the establishment of the Reformation in England, and the destruction of the monasteries. His six marriages and three more or less legitimate children have been widely chronicled. Died in 1547.

(From MS. B.M. Additional 31922, edited by Flügel in *Anglia* XII; spelling modernised.)

Pastime with good company
I love and shall until I die.
Grudge who lust, but none deny,
So God be pleased thus live will I.
For my pastance
Hunt, sing and dance,
My heart is set.
All goodly sport
For my comfort—
Who shall me let?

Youth must have some dalliance,
Of good or ill some pastance.
Company me thinks the best,
All thoughts and fancies to digest,
For idleness
Is chief mistress
Of vices all—
Then who can say
But mirth and play
Is best of all?

Company with honesty
Is virtue—vices to flee.
Company is good and ill,
But every man hath his free will.
The best ensue,
The worst eschew,
My mind shall be;
Virtue to use,
Vice to refuse,
Thus shall I use me.

let, *prevent.*
ensue, *follow.*

Quatrain

O my heart and o my heart,
My heart it is so sore,
Since I must needs from my love depart
And know no cause wherefore.

A Refrain

Alack, alack, what shall I do?
For care is cast into my heart,
And true love locked thereto.
    (sung three times over)

Green groweth the holly

Green groweth the holly, so doth the ivy.
Though winter blasts blow never so high,
Green groweth the holly.

As the holly groweth green
And never changeth hue,
So am I, ever have been,
Unto my lady true.
              (*chorus*)

As the holly groweth green
With ivy all alone,
When flowers can not be seen,
And green wood leaves be gone.
              (*chorus*)

Now unto my lady
Promise to her I make
From all other only
To her I me betake.
              (*chorus*)

Adieu mine own lady,
Adieu my special,
Who hath my heart truly,
Be sure, and ever shall.

(chorus)

Whereto should I express

Whereto should I express
My inward heaviness?
No mirth can make me fain
Till that we meet again.

Do way, dear heart, not so;
Let no thought you dismay
Though ye now part me fro;
We shall meet when we may.

When I remember me
Of your most gentle mind,
It may in no wise agree
That I should be unkind.

The daisy delectable,
The violet wan and blo,
Ye are not variable—
I love you and no mo.

I make you fast and sure,
It is to me great pain,
Thus long to endure
Till that we meet again.

blo, *pallid*.

Without discord

Without discord
and both accord
   now let us be;
both hearts alone
to set in one
   best seemeth me.

For when one soul
is in the dole
   of lovës pain,
then help must have
himself to save
   and love to obtain.

Wherefore now we
that lovers be,
   let us now pray,
once love sure
for to procure,
   without denay.

Where love so sueth
there no heart rueth,
   but condescend;
if contrary,
what remedy?
   God it amend.

dole, *grief*.

Though some say

Though some say that youth ruleth me,
I trust in age for to tarry;
God and my right and my duty,
From them shall I never vary,
Though some say that youth ruleth me.
                              (repeat)

I pray you all that aged be,
How well did ye your youth carry?
I think some wars of each degree;
There in a wager lay dare I,
Though some say that youth ruleth me.

(repeat verse 1)

Pastimes of youth some time among
None can say but necessary;
I hurt no man, I do no wrong,
I love true where I did marry,
Though some say that youth ruleth me.

(repeat this verse)

Then soon discuss that hence we must,
Pray we to God and Saint Mary
That all amend, and here an end,
Thus saith the King the eighth Harry,
Though some say that youth ruleth me.
I hurt no man, I do no wrong,
I love truly where I did marry,
Though some say that youth ruleth me.

Whoso that will for grace sue

Whoso that will for grace sue,
his intent must needs be true
and love her in heart and deed;
else it were pity that he should speed.
Many one saith that love is ill,
but those be they which can no skill.

Or else because they may not obtain,
they would that other should it disdain.
But love is a thing given by God,
in that therefore can be none odd,
but perfect in deed and between two;
wherefore then should we it eschew?

EDWARD VI

Son of Henry VIII by his third wife, Jane Seymour. Became King at the age of nine and died in 1553 at the age of fifteen, from the combined effects of several illnesses and an attempt to treat them with arsenic. A cold, intellectual, unsympathetic child, deeply interested in Protestant theology.

His only known poem, addressed to Sir Anthony Seyntleger, Knight of
his privy chamber.

In Eucharist then there is bread,
Whereto I do consent:
Then with bread is our bodyes fed;
But farther what is ment?
I say that Christ in flesh and blood
Is there continually;
Unto our soule a speciall food,
Taking it spiritually.
And this transubstantiation I
Beleeve as I have read:
That Christ sacramentally
Is there in forme of bread.
S.Austen sayth the Word doth come
Unto the element:
And there is made, he sayth in somme,
A perfect sacrament.
The element then doth remaine,
Or els must needes ensue:
S.Austen's words be nothing plaine,
Nor cannot be found true.
For if the Word, as he doth say,
Come to the element:
Then is not the element away,
But bides there verament.
Yet who so eateth that lively food,
And hath a perfect faith:
Receiveth Christes flesh and bloud,
For Christ himself so saith.
Not with our teeth his flesh to teare,
Nor take bloud for our drink:
Too great absurditie it were
So grossely for to thinke.
For we must eate him spiritually,
If we be spirituall:
And who so eates him carnally,
Thereby shall have a fall.

For he is now a spirituall meate,
And spiritually we must
That spirituall meate spiritually eate,
And leave our carnall lust.
Thus by the spirit I spiritually
Beleeve, say what men list:
None other transubstantiation I
Beleeve of the Eucharist,
But that there is both bread and wine,
Which we see with our eye:
Yet Christ is there by power divine,
To those that spiritually
Do eate that bread and drinke that cup,
Esteeming it but light:
As Judas did, which eate that sop,
Not judging it aright.
For I was taught not long agone,
I should leane to the spirit:
And let the carnall flesh alone,
For it did not profite.
God save him that teaching me taught,
For I thereby did winne:
To put me from that carnall thought
That I before was in.
For I beleeve Christ corporally
In heaven doth keepe his place:
And yet Christ sacramentally
Is heere with us by grace.
So that, in this high mysterie,
We must eate spirituall meate,
To keepe his death in memory,
Least we should it forget.
This do I say, this have I sayd,
This saying say will I:
This saying though I once denaid,
I will no more to dye.

LADY JANE GREY

Born in 1537, the eldest daughter of Henry Grey, Duke of Suffolk, and great-granddaughter of Henry VII. She was proclaimed Queen on the death of her cousin, Edward VI, who had been persuaded to name her as his successor in his will, but only reigned nine days. She and her husband, Lord Guildford Dudley, were imprisoned in the Tower by the victorious sovereign, Mary I, and after the Wyatt rebellion were beheaded (1554), largely because Philip of Spain had insisted on the removal of such potentially dangerous rivals before he would marry Mary. Lady Jane was the figurehead of the extreme Protestant party, a very learned, quiet and serious girl, and the victim of other people's dynastic and political ambitions.

Ballard, in his *Memoirs of Several Ladies* of 1752, says of Lady Jane Grey,

'While she was in durance she wrote the following latin verses with a Pin:

> Non aliena putes homini, quae obtingere possunt,
> Sors hodierna mihi, tunc erit illa tibi.
>> JANE DUDLEY.

> Deo juvante, nil nocet livor malus:
> Et non juvante, non juvat labor Gravis.
>> Post tenebras spero lucem.'

Do not think that anything which can happen is foreign to mankind; the fate that is mine today may be yours tomorrow.

When God helps us, evil envy does us no harm; if he helps us not, our toil is useless.

After darkness I hope for light.

ELIZABETH I

Born in 1533, daughter of Henry VIII by his second wife Anne Bullen, and considered illegitimate, heretical, and generally dangerous for most of her youth. Came to the throne at the age of twenty-five, having narrowly escaped death as a traitor in her sister's reign. Her own rule is associated with the rise of England as a European power, the defeat of the Armada, and the rich development of English literature. She died in 1603.

i) 'O stelliferi conditor orbis'

O framar of starry circle,
Who lening to the lasting grounstone
Withe whorling blast hevens turnest,
And Law compelst the skies to beare:
Now that with ful horne,
Meting all her brothers flames
The lessar stars the mone dimmes,
Now darke and pale her horne,
Nar to Son loseth her light.
And she that at beginning of night,
Hesperus frosen rising makes,
And Luciphar palled by Phoebus upriseth,
Againe her wonted raines exchangeth.
Thou, by the cold of lefe falne shade
Straightist thy light with shortar abode:
Thou whan the fervent sommar comes,
Easy nights houres devidest.
Thy power tempers the changing year,
That what leves Boreas blastz bereves,
Gentil Sephirus brings as fast:
Sedes that the Northe star doth behold,
At hiest blade the dok star burnith up.
Naught loused from auncient Law
Leves the worke of her owne place.
Al giding with assured end,
Mans workes alone thou dost dispice.
O gidar by right desart from meane to kipe.

dok star, *Sirius.*

For why so many slipar fortune
Turnes doth make? Oppressing faultles
Dew paine for wicked mete,
But in hy seatz the wicked factz abide,
And wicked stamps on holy necks with uniust turne.
And cleare vertu dimmed
With thick blackness lurketh,
And iust man the wickeds crime doth beare.
Fals othe in fraude doth the annoy.
Who when the[y] can use ther forse,
Whom many vulgar feare
The mightiest kings the[y] can subdue.
O now behold of wretched erthe,
Thou who so ties the bondz of all.
Us men regard of thy great worke not the vilest part,
How tost we be with fortunes waves.
O weldar apeace the roring floudes,
And with what boundz the great heaven thou gidest
                        the stable erthe do stedy.

ii) 'Nubibus atris'. This is taken from the Queen's autograph MS.

Dim Cloudes
Sky Close
Light none
Can afourd.
If Roling Seas
boustius Sowth
Mixe his fome,
Griny ons
Like the Clirristz
days the water
straight moude
sturd up al foule
the Sight gainsais.

griny, *bluish-green.*
moude, *mud.*

Running streame
that poures
from hiest hilz
Oft is staid
by Slaked
stone of Rock.
thou, if thou wilt
in Clirest Light
trothe behold,
by straight lin
hit in the pathe:
Chase Joyes,
repulse feare,
thrust out hope,
Wo not retaine.
Cloudy is the mind
With snafle bound,
Wher they reign.

iii) 'Cum polo Phoebus'

In poole whan Phebus with reddy waine
the light to spred begins,
The star dimed with flames opprissing,
Pales her whitty lookes.
Whan wood with Siphirus mildding blast
blusheth with the springing Roses,
And clowdy Sowthe his blustering blastes;
Away from stauke the beauty goes.
Some time with calmy fayre, the se
Void of waves doth run,
Oft boistrus tempestz the North
With foming Seas turnes up.
If rarely stedy be the worldz forme,
If turnes so many hit makes,
Belive slippar mens Luckes,
trust that sliding be ther goodz.
Certain, and in Eternal Law is writ,
'Sure standeth naugh is made'.

stauke, *thorns*.
reddy waine, *rosy chariot*.

iv) 'Felix nimium prior aetas' (*spelling modernised*)

Happy too much the former age
With faithful field content,
Not lost by sluggish lust,
That wonts not the long fasts
To loose by soon-got acorn,
That knew not Bacchus' gifts
With molten honey mixed.
Nor Serian shining fleece
With Tyrian venom dyed.
Sound sleeps gave the grass,
Their drink the running stream,
Shades gave the highest pine.
The depth of the sea they fathomed not,
Nor wares chosen from far
Made stranger find new shores.
Then were navies still,
Nor bloodshed by cruel hate
Had fearful weapons stained.
What first fury to foes should
Any arms raise,
When cruel wounds he saw
And no reward for blood?
Would God again our former time
To wonted manners fell,
But greedy getting love burns
Sorer than Etna with her flames.
O who the first man was
Of hidden gold the weight
Or gems that willing lurked
The dear danger digged?

v) 'Quicumque solam mente praecipiti'

Who so with hedlong mind glory
Alone believes as greatest thing,
And quarters of largist hevens behold
With straightid seat of erthe,
Wyl blusche that hit not filz
The short compas of gridy desire.
Why proude men do you crake
Your necks from mortal yoke retire?
Thogh fame by people strange
Flying spred the tonges open
And noble house by great titelz shine:
Dethe hates the hiest glory,
Intangels low and hauty hed,
And equalz lest to most.
Wher now lies faithful Fabritius bones?
Wher Brutus or currish Cato?
Smal lasting fame signes
A vaine name with fewest lettars.
But why do we knowe noble names,
Do we not see them to consumed?
Ly you shal unknowen at all
Nor fame shal uttar Who.
If you suppose that life be longar drawen
For brethe of mortal fame,
Than the second dethe exspect.

l. 7, crake, *boast*
l. 25, Than, *Then*

34

vi) 'Eheu quae miseros'

O in how begiling pathe
Men Ignorance leades.
Seake not the golde in griny tre
Nor louke for precious stone on grape,
Hide not on hily tops your baites,
Your dische with fische to fil;
And gotes if thou wylt take,
The Tyrrhene Sea not serche.
For hid in the waves man knoes the waters streame,
And what fiersist river have whittist pearle
Or wher the reddys rubies
And shores also fild most with smallist fische
Or have most porpos skales.
But hiden for they know not
The Good the[y] seake,
Blindid ignorant must the[y] bide,
To cerche byonde the Northen Pole,
Drowned in the erthe the[y] rake.
What hest shall I for dullardz make?
Even this that whan with carke the falz have got,
Truist than shalt knowe
                    the best.

l. 10 fiersist; the Queen has translated *feracior* (more fruitful) as *ferocior*.
l. 20 carke, *hard work*.
l. 21 than, *then*.

vii) 'Felix qui potuit boni'

Blist, that may of Good
The fontaine clire behold,
Happy that can of waighty
Erthe the bondes to breake.
The Tracian profit wons
His wives funeralz wailing
Whan with sorrows note
The wavering trees he moved,
And stedy rivers made,
And hind caused join
Unfearing sides to lion fierce.
Nor hare did feare the looke
Of cruel dog so plised with song,
Whan ferventar desir the inward
Brest more burnt,
Nor could the notes that al subdued
Pacefie ther lord,
Of ireful Godz complaining
The helly house went to.
Ther faining verse
Tuning to sounding stringe
What he drew from springes
The greatest of Mother Godz,
What feable mone could give,
What doubled love afourd,
By wailes and hel doth stur
And with dulce suite pardon
Of darkenes Lorde besiche.
Wondar doth the thre hedded
Jailor amasid with unwonted verse,
Revenging Goddes of faultes
That wontid gilty feare
Sorrowing with teares bedewed the[y] were.

l. 5 wons, *once long ago*.

36

Not Ixiones hed
The whirling while did turne
And lost with longue thirst
Tantalus rivers skornes.
The vultur fild with notes,
Tityus livor tared not.
At last wailing said the juge
Of shady place, 'we yeld;
To man we give his wife for feere,
Won by his song.
With this law be bound the gift,
While in the Tartar thou bidest,
Turne back thy looke thou must not'.
But who to Love gives law?
For greatest law his love he made.
So night drawing to her ende,
Eurydicen his Orpheus
Sawe, lost, and killed.
This fable toucheth you
Who so doth seak to gide
To hiest day his mynd.
For who in hely shade
Won man his yees doth bend,
What so he chifest held
In vewing hel hathe 'ost.

l. 35 while, *wheel.*
l. 42 feere, *companion.*
l. 55 in hely shade, *into the cave of Hell.*
l. 56 won man, *being overcome*; yees, *eyes.*

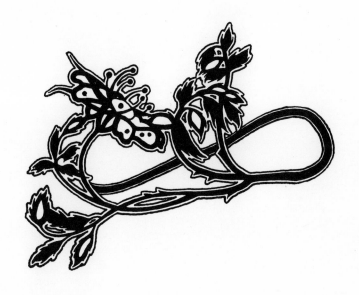

PORTRAITS

Henry VI

Edward VI

Lady Jane Grey

Elizabeth I

James I of Scotland

Mary Queen of Scots

Henry Lord Darnley

The Queen also translated Horace's *Ars Poetica*, and 123 lines of Seneca's *Hercules in Oeta*; the latter can be found in MS. e Musaeo 55. I now give four of her own poems, the second two being only attributed to her, but quite probably genuine. Their spelling is modernised.

Poem written c. 1584, about Mary Queen of Scots (?)

The doubt of future foes exiles my present joy,
And wit me warns to shun such snares as threaten mine annoy;
For falsehood now doth flow and subjects' faith doth ebb,
Which should not be if reason ruled or wisdom weaved the web.
But clouds of joys untried do cloak aspiring minds,
Which turn to rain of late repent by changed course of winds.
The top of hope suppressed the root upreared shall be,
And fruitless all their grafted guile, as shortly you shall see.
The dazzled eyes with pride, which great ambition blinds,
Shall be unsealed by worthy wights whose foresight falsehood finds.
The daughter of debate that discord aye doth sow
Shall reap no gain where former rule still peace hath taught to know.
No foreign banished wight shall anchor in this port;
Our realm brooks not sedition's sects, let them elsewhere resort.
My rusty sword through rest shall first his edge employ
To poll their tops that seek such change or gape for future joy.

Love Poem

I grieve and dare not show my discontent,
I love and yet am forced to seem to hate,
I do, yet dare not say I ever meant,
I seem stark mute but inwardly do prate.
    I am and not, I freeze and yet am burned
    Since from myself my other self I turned.

My care is like my shadow in the sun,
Follows me flying, flies when I pursue it,
Stands and lies by me, doth what I have done.
His too familiar care doth make me rue it.
    No means I find to rid him from my breast,
    Till by the end of things it be supprest.

Some gentler passions slide into my mind,
For I am soft and made of melting snow;
Or be more cruel, love, and so be kind.
Let me or float or sink, be high or low.
    Or let me live with some more sweet content,
    Or die and so forget what love e'er meant.

Elizabeth's Answer to a Popish Priest who pressed her to declare her opinion concerning the Corporal Presence.

Christ was the word that spake it,
He took the bread and brake it,
And what that word did make it,
That I believe and take it.

When I was fair and young, and favour gracèd me,
Of many was I sought, their mistress for to be;
But I did scorn them all, and answered them therefore,
    'Go, go, go, seek some otherwhere,
    Importune me no more!'

How many weeping eyes I made to pine with woe,
How many sighing hearts, I have no skill to show;
Yet I the prouder grew, and answered them therefore,
    'Go, go, go, seek some otherwhere,
    Importune me no more!'

Then spake fair Venus' son, that proud victorious boy,
And said, 'Fine Dame, since that you be so coy,
I will so pluck your plumes that you shall say no more,
    Go, go, go, seek some otherwhere,
    Importune me no more!'

When he had spake these words, such change grew in my breast
That neither night nor day since that, I could take any rest.
Then lo, I did repent that I had said before,
    'Go, go, go, seek some otherwhere,
    Importune me no more!'

JAMES VI and I

Born in 1566, son of Mary Queen of Scots and Lord Darnley. Became King of Scotland at the age of thirteen months, when his mother was forced to abdicate (or in 1587, when she was beheaded), and King of England in 1603, on the death of Elizabeth. A shabby, nervous man, very proud of his poetic gifts and of his theological learning. Patron of the Authorised Version of the Bible, nearly victim of the Gunpowder Plot, and described by Henri IV of France as 'the wisest fool in Christendom'. Married Anne of Denmark. Died in 1625, and was succeeded by his second son, Charles, the eldest, Henry, having predeceased him.

From *The Essays of a Prentise*, published 1584

Sonnet 3, Invocation

And first, ô *Phoebus*, when I do descrive
The *Springtyme* sproutar of the herbes and flowris,
Whomewith in rank none of the foure do strive,
But nearest thee do stande all tymes and howris:
Graunt Readers may esteme, they sie the showris,
Whose balmie dropps so softlie dois distell,
Which watrie cloudds in mesure suche downe powris,
As makis the herbis, and verie earth to smell
With savours sweit, fra tyme that onis thy sell
The vapouris softlie sowkis with smyling cheare,
Whilks syne in cloudds are keiped closs and well,
Whill vehement Winter come in tyme of yeare.
   Graunt, when I lyke the *Springtyme* to displaye,
    That Readers think they sie the Spring alwaye.

Sonnet 6

But let them think, in verie deid they feill,
Whan as I do the *Winters* stormes unfolde,
The bitter frosts, which waters dois congeill
In *Winter* season, by a pearcing colde.
And that they heare the whiddering *Boreas* bolde,
With hiddeous hurling, rolling Rocks from hie.
Or let them think, they see god *Saturne* olde,
Whose hoarie haire owercovering earth, maks flie
The lytle birds in flocks, fra tyme they see
The earth and all with stormes of snow owercled:
Yea let them think, they heare the birds that die,
Make piteous mone, that *Saturnes* hairis are spred.
   Apollo, graunt thir foirsaid suitis of myne,
    All fyne I say, that thou may crowne me syne.

With other sonnets, this book also contains a translation of du Bartas'
Uranie, and a long poem, *Ane Metaphoricall Invention of a Tragedie called
Phoenix*. The King's next book, *His majesties poeticall exercises at vacant
houres*, published in 1591, consists of another translation from du Bartas,
The Furies, a long narrative poem, *The Lepanto*, and this final sonnet:

The azur'd vaulte, the crystall circles bright,
The gleaming fyrie torches powdred there,
The changing round, the shyning beamie light,
The sad and bearded fyres, the monsters faire:
The prodiges appearing in the aire,
The rearding thunders, and the blustering winds,
The foules, in hew, in shape, in nature raire,
The prettie notes that wing'd musiciens finds:
In earth the sav'rie floures, the mettal'd minds,
The wholesome hearbes, the hautie pleasant trees,
The sylver streames, the beasts of sundrie kinds,
The bounded roares and fishes of the seas:
   All these, for teaching man, the LORD did frame,
   To do his will, whose glorie shines in thame.

I.R.S.

rearding, *roaring*.
minds, *mines*.
roares, *noises*.

There are a number of Psalms rendered into English verse by the
King in MS. Royal 18.B.xvi; and MS. B.M.Add.24195, written *c.*
1616–18, contains *All the kings short poesis that ar not printed*: from it the
next three poems come.

A complaint against the contrary Wyndes that hindered the Queene to com to Scotland from Denmarke. (Written in 1589.)

From sacred throne in heaven Empyrick hie
A breathe divine in Poëts brests does blowe
Wherethrough all things inferiour in degrie
As vassalls unto them doe hommage showe
There songs enchants Apollos selfe ye knowe
And chaste Dianas coache can haste or staye
Can change the course of Planets high or lowe
And make the earthe obeye them everie waye
Make rockes to danse, hugge hills to skippe and playe
Beasts, foules, and fishe to followe them allwhere
Though thus the heaven, the sea, and earthe obeye,
Yett mutins the midde region of the aire.
   What hatefull Juno, Aeolus entiseth
   Whereby contrarious Zephyre thus ariseth.

A sonnet on Tycho Brahe, whom the King visited at Uraniborg in 1590.

The glorious globe of heavenlie matter made
Containing ten celestiall circles faire
Where shining starres in glistring graithe arraide
Most pleasantlie are poudered here and thair
Where everie planet hath his owen repaire
And christall house, a whirling wheill in rounde
Whose calme aspects or froward does declaire
Gods minde to blisse great kingdomes or confounde
Then if you list to see on earthlie grounde
There ordour, course, and influence appeare
Looke Tichoes tooles, there finelie shall be founde
Each planet dansing in his propre spheare
   There fires divine into his house remaine
   Whome sommerlie his booke doth here containe.

graithe, *splendour.*
sommerlie, *fully.*

Song, the first verses that ever the King made (that is, in 1582, at the age of fifteen).

Since thought is free, thinke what thou will
O troubled hart to ease thy paine
Thought unrevealed can doe no evill
Bot wordes past out, cummes not againe
    Be cairefull aye for to invent
    The waye to gett thy owen intent.

To pleas thy selfe with thy concaite
And lett none knowe what thou does meane
Houpe ay at last, though it be late
To thy intent for to attaine
    Thoght whiles it brake forth in effect
    Yet aye lett witt thy will correct.

Since foole haste cumes not greatest speede
I wold thou shoulde learne for to knaw
How to make vertue of a neede
Since that necessitie hath no law
    With patience then see thou attend
    And houpe to vanquise in the end.

An Epitaph on Sir Philip Sidney, published in the Cambridge volume of memorial verses, Academiae Cantabrigiensis Lachrymae, *in 1587.*

Thou mighty *Mars* the Lord of Souldiers brave,
And thou, *Minerve*, that dois in witt excell,
And thou *Apollo* who dois knowledge have
Of every art that from *Parnassus* fell
With all your *Sisters* that thaireon do dwell,
Lament for him, who duelie serv'd you all
Whome in you wisely all your arts did mell,
Bewaile (I say) his inexspected fall,
I neede not in remembrance for to call
His race, his youth, the hope had of him ay
Since that in him doth cruell death appall
Both manhood, wit, and learning every way,
    Bot yet he doth in bed of *honor* rest,
    And evermore of him shall live the best.

mell, *mingle.*

On the death of his wife Queen Anne, in 1619.

Thee to invite the great God sent a star,
Whose nearest friends and kin good Princes are;
For though they run the race of men and die,
Death serves but to refine their majesty.
So did my queen from hence her court remove,
And left the earth to be enthroned above.
Thus she is changed, not dead; no good Prince dies,
But like the day-star only sets to rise.

CHARLES I

Born in 1600. Became King in 1625, and from the very beginning found himself in conflict with Parliament and in great need of money. These difficulties increased, leading to the Civil War, and finally to the execution of the King on January 30, 1649. Married the French King's daughter, Henriette Marie, who returned to France during the troubles and kept alive a threadbare English court in exile while the Puritans ruled in England.

Poem written from Carisbrooke, 1648. Both the title, 'Majesty in Misery', the variations, and some manifestly false verses I have omitted, I suspect of having been added by some pious forger after the King's death, for propaganda probably.

Great monarch of the world, from whose arm springs
The potency and power of kings,
Record the royal woe, my sufferings.

Nature and law, by thy divine decree,
(The only root of righteous royalty)
With this dim diadem invested me;

With it the sacred sceptre, purple robe,
Thy holy unction, and the royal globe;
Yet I am levelled with the life of Job.

The fiercest furies that do daily tread
Upon my grief, my gray discrowned head,
Are those that to my bounty owe their bread.

Tyranny bears the title of taxation,
Revenge and robbery are reformation,
Oppression gains the name of sequestration.

Great Britain's heir is forcéd into France,
Whilst on his father's head his foes advance;
Poor child, he weeps out his inheritance.

With my own power my majesty they wound;
In the king's name, the king himself's uncrown'd;
So doth the dust destroy the diamond.

My life they prize at such a slender rate
That in my absence they draw bills of hate
To prove the King a traitor to the State.

Felons obtain more privilege than I,
They are allowed to answer ere they die.
'Tis death to me to ask the reason why.

But sacred Saviour, with thy words I woo
Thee *to forgive*, and not be bitter to
Such as thou know'st *do not know what they do*.

Augment my patience, nullify my hate,
Preserve my issue, and inspire my mate;
Yet, though we perish, bless this Church and State!

    It seems unlikely that in this guise the poem is all by the King; the direct reference to the Passion smacks more of the Martyr-King cult than of a personal poem, in which it would seem to a man like Charles an impossible blasphemy. Most likely the poem has been worked up from an original poem by the King in order to revive, or to keep alive, Royalist feeling. This is based on the text in Chalmers' *Poetic Remains of the Scotish Kings*; some verses are quoted in d'Israeli's *Curiosities of Literature*, and there is plenty more, some of it obviously interpolations, in the mid-eighteenth-century *Reliquiae Sacrae Carolinae*.

CHARLES II

Son of Charles I and Henriette Marie, born in 1630. Nominally commanded the Royalist forces in the West during the Civil War. Crowned King of Scotland in 1651, and King of England on his Restoration in 1660. Married Catherine of Braganza, but had no legitimate children (though dozens of the other kind). Easy-going, familiar and dissipated in his manners, witty, and a great patron of the arts, especially music. Died in 1685 and was succeeded by his brother, James II.

To Lady Frances Stewart, 1663.

I pass all my hours in a shady old grove,
But I live not the day when I see not my love;
I survey every walk now my Phillis is gone,
And sigh when I think we were there all alone.
   O then 'tis, O then, that I think there's no hell
   Like loving, like loving too well.

While alone to myself I repeat all her charms,
She I love may be locked in another man's arms;
She may laugh at my cares and so false she may be
To say all the kind things she before said to me:
   O then 'tis, O then, that I think there's no hell
   Like loving too well.

But when I consider the truth of her heart,
Such an innocent passion, so kind without art,
I fear I have wronged her, and hope she may be
So full of true love to be jealous of me;
   And then 'tis I think that no joys be above
   The pleasures of love.

FREDERICK PRINCE OF WALES

Son of George II and father of George III. Born in 1707. Always cordially detested by his family. His mother is recorded to have said of him, 'My dear firstborn is the greatest ass, and the greatest liar, and the greatest *canaille*, and the greatest beast in the whole world, and I heartily wish he was out of it.' Married his cousin Augusta of Saxe-Gotha, and died in 1751, nine years before his father.

This unusual Hanoverian, who would have been King but for his premature death, wrote the following two poems, both in acquired languages, his native tongue being German, the first dedicated to his wife, and the second to the Ladies Hanmer, Falconberg, and Middlesex, who acted with him in Congreve's *Judgement of Paris*.

The Charms of Sylvia

'Tis not the liquid brightness of those eyes,
That swim with pleasure and delight,
Nor those heavenly arches which arise
O'er each of them to shade their light:
'Tis not that hair which plays with every wind,
And loves to wanton round thy face;
Now straying round the forehead, now behind
Retiring with insidious grace.
'Tis not that lovely range of teeth so white,
As new-shorn sheep equal and fair;
Nor e'en that gentle smile, the heart's delight,
With which no smile could e'er compare.
'Tis not that chin so round, that neck so fine,
Those breasts that swell to meet my love,
That easy sloping waist, that form divine,
Nor ought below, nor ought above:
'Tis not the living colours over each
By nature's finest pencil wrought,
To shame the full-blown rose, and blooming peach,
And mock the happy painter's thought:
No—'tis that gentleness of mind, that love
So kindly answering my desire;
That grace with which you look, and speak, and move,
That thus has set my soul on fire.

Venez, mes cheres Deesses,
Venez calmer mon chagrin;
Aidez, mes belles Princesses,
A le noyer dans le vin.
Poussons cette douce ivresse
Jusqu'au milieu de la nuit,
Et n'ecoutons que la tendresse
D'un charmant vis-à-vis.
Quand le chagrin me devore,
Vite à table je me mets,
Loin des objets que j'abhorre,
Avec joie j'y trouve la paix.
Peu d'amis, restes d'un naufrage,
Je rassemble autour de moi,
Et je me ris de l'etalage
Qu'a chez lui toujours un Roi.
Que m'importe que l'Europe
Ait un ou plusieurs tyrans?
Prions seulement Calliope
Qu'elle inspire nos vers, nos chants;
Laissons Mars et toute la gloire,
Livrons nous tous à l'amour;
Que Bacchus nous donne à boire;
A ces deux faisons la cour.
Passons ainsi notre vie,
Sans rêver à ce qui suit,
Avec ma chere Silvie
Le tems trop vite me fuit.
Mais si par un malheur extrême,
Je perdois cet objet charmant;
Qui, cette compagnie même
Ne me tiendroit un moment,
Me livrant à ma tristesse,
Toujours plein de mon chagrin,
Je n'aurois plus d'allegresse
Pour mettre Bathurst en train.
Ainsi pour vous tenir en joie,
Invoquez toujours les Dieux,
Qu'elle vive et qu'elle soit
Avec nous toujours heureux.

Come, my dear Goddesses, to calm my disappointment; help me, fair Princesses, to drown it in wine. Continue this sweet intoxication far into the night, listening only to the tenderness of a charming companion. When unhappiness overcomes me, straightway I sit down to the table, and far from the objects I detest, joyfully there I find peace. I collect around me my few friends, relics of my shipwreck, and laugh at the pomp that must always surround a King. What does it matter to me that Europe has one or several tyrants? Let us simply pray the Muse to inspire our songs and verses. Let us ignore Mars and all his glory, devoting ourselves entirely to love; let Bacchus pour our drink, and let us court no deity but these two. Let us spend our life thus, without dreaming of what is to follow; with my dear Sylvia, time flies too quickly. But if by some extreme misfortune I were to lose that charming lady, even this company could not keep me for a moment; I should give myself up to misery, forever full of despair, should have no more delight in quizzing and joking with Bathurst. So, to keep yourselves in joy, invoke the Gods always, asking that she may live and remain ever happy with us.

GEORGE IV

Eldest son of George III and Charlotte of Mecklenburg-Strelitz. Born 1762. Acted as Prince Regent during his father's periods of madness. Achieved quite a reputation as a dandy and a rake, and probably contracted a morganatic and illegal marriage with the Roman Catholic Mrs. Fitzherbert. Married his cousin Caroline of Brunswick-Wolfenbuttel, whom he treated odiously (although it must be admitted that the lady was given to rather indiscreet and embarrassing scenes herself). Came to the throne in 1820, and died of dropsy, gout, etc., in 1830. His only child, the Princess Charlotte, died in childbirth in 1817, and Prinny was succeeded by his brother, William IV.

Oh! Campbell, the scene of tonight
Has open'd the wound of my heart;
It has shown me how great the delight
Which the charms of thy converse impart.
I've known what it is to be gay,
I've revell'd in joy's fleeting hour,
I've wish'd for the close of the day,
To meet in a thick-woven bower.

'Twas there that the soft-stolen kiss,
'Twas there that the throb of our hearts,
Betray'd that we wished for the bliss
Which love, and love only, imparts.
But Fate will those hearts oft dissever,
By Nature design'd for each other;
But why should they part? and for ever!
And forced their affections to smother.

How short and how blissful the hour
When round each lone hamlet we stray'd;
When passion each heart could o'erpower,
And a sigh the sweet feelings betray'd.
O whence is that glance of the mind
Which scenes that are past oft renews;
Which shows them, in colours refined
With fancy's bright glitt'ring hues?

Now, sweet be thy slumbers, my friend,
And sweet be the dreams of thy soul;
Around thee may angels attend,
And visions of happiness roll.
Whilst I——

(*the rest is prudently omitted in the printed version I saw*)

JAMES I OF SCOTLAND

Born in 1394. Captured at sea by the English in 1405. Imprisoned in the Tower and various other State prisons. Became King of Scotland on the death of his father, Robert III, in 1406. Married the Lady Joan Beaufort and was released to return to his own kingdom in February 1423/4. Murdered in February 1436/7, and succeeded by his son, James II. He wrote the long and beautiful poem, the 'Kingis Quair' ('The King's Book') in captivity at Windsor in 1423, and is credited also with the jolly ballad, 'Peebles to the Play', a description of the sports at a country fair, which may have been written by James V, with a 'Song on Absence' and the hymn, 'Sen throw Vertew'.

Sen throw vertew incressis dignitie,
And vertew is flour and rute of nobles ay,
Of ony wit, or quhat estait thou be
His steppis follow, and dreid for none effray;
Exil al vice, and follow treuth alway;
Lufe maist thy God, that first thy lufe began,
And for ilk inche He will the quyte ane span.

Be not ouir proude in thy prosperitie,
For as it cummis, sa will it pas away;
The tyme to compt is schort, thou may weill se,
For of grene gress sone cummis wallowit hay.
Labour in treuth, quhilk suith is of thy fay,
Traist maist in God, for He best gyde the can,
And for ilk inche He will the quyte a span.

Sen word is thrall, and thocht is only fre
Thou dant thy toung, that power hes and may,
Thou steik thy ene fra warldis vanitie,
Refraine thy lust, and harkin quhat I say:
Graip or thou slyde, and keip furth the hie way,
Thou hald the fast upon thy God and man,
And for ilk inche He will the quyte ane span.

nobles, *nobility.*
quhilk suith is of thy fay, *which is the pledge of thy faith.*
dant, *tame.*
ene, *eyes.*
ilk, *every.*

The poet lies awake all night, thinking 'of many diverse thing'; he reads some Boethius and meditates on the changes of Fortune, until the morning comes. He resolves to write a poem, and begins to describe his own misfortune, his youth, and his kidnapping by the English.

Quhare as In ward full oft I wold bewaille
My dedely lyf, full of peyne and penance,
Saing ryght thus, quhat have I gilt to faille
My fredome in this warld and my plesance?
Sen every wight has thereof suffisance,
That I behold, and I a creature
Put from all this—hard Is myn aventure!

The bird, the beste, the fisch eke In the see,
They lyve in fredome everich In his kynd;
And I a man, and lakkith libertee;
Quhat schall I seyne, quhat resoun may I fynd,
That fortune suld do so? thus In my mynd
My folk I wold argewe, bot all for noght;
Was non that myght, that on my peynes rought.

Than wold I say, 'gif god me had devisit
To lyve my lyf in thraldome thus and pyne,
Quhat was the cause that he me more comprisit
Than othir folke to lyve in suich ruyne?
I suffer allone amang the figuris nyne,
Ane wofull wrecche that to no wight may spede,
And yit of every lyvis help hath nede.'

quhat have I gilt to faille, *what have I done wrong that I should lose?*
everich, *each one.*
amang the figuris nyne—*he is comparing himself to a cypher in arithmetic.*
spede, *be of help.*
lyvis, *living person's.*

The longë dayes and the nightis eke
I wold bewaille my fortune in this wise,
For quhich, agane distresse confort to seke,
My custum was on mornis for to ryse
Airly as day; o happy excercise!
By the come I to Ioye out of turmente.
Bot now to purpose of my first entent:

Bewailing In my chamber thus allone,
Despeired of all Ioye and remedye,
For-tirit of my thoght, and wo-begone,
Unto the wyndow gan I walk In hye,
To se the warld and folk that went forby;
As for the tyme, though I of myrthis fude
Myght have no more, to luke It did me gude.

Now was there maid fast by the touris wall
A gardyn faire, and in the corneris set
Ane herbere grene, with wandis long and small
Railit about; and so with treis set
Was all the place, and hawthorn hegis knot,
That lyf was non walking there forby,
That myght within scarse ony wight aspye.

So thik the bewis and the leves grene
Beschadit all the aleyes that there were,
And myddis every herebere myght be sene
The scharpë grenë suetë Jenepere,
Growing so faire with branchis here and there,
That, as It semyt to a lyf without,
The bewis spred the herbere all about.

By the come I, *by thee I came.*
For-tirit of, *wearied out by.*
In hye, *in haste.*
small, *slender.*
lyf, *person.*
bewis, *boughs.*

And on the smallë grenë twistis sat
The lytill suetë nightingale, and song
So loud and clere, the ympnis consecrat
Off lufis use, now soft, now lowd among,
That all the gardyng and the wallis rong
Ryght of thaire song, and on the copill next
Off thaire suete armony, and lo the text:

'Worschippe, ye that loveris bene, this may,
For of your blisse the kalendis are begonne,
And sing with us, away, winter, away!
Cum, somer, cum, the suete sesoun and sonne!
Awake for schame! that have your hevynis wonne,
And amorously lift up your hedis all,
Thank lufe that list you to his merci call.'

Quhen thai this song had song a lytill thrawe,
Thai stent a quhile, and therewith unaffraid,
As I beheld and kest myn eyne a-lawe,
From beugh to beugh thay hippit and thai plaid,
And freschely in thaire birdis kynd arraid
Thaire fetheris new, and fret thame In the sonne,
And thankit lufe, that had thaire makis wonne.

ympnis off luvis use, *hymns from the service-book of Love.*
copill, *couplet, verse.*
hevynis, *heavens.*
thrawe, *while, time.*
stent, *stopped.*
kest myn eyne a-lawe, *looked down.*
hippit, *hopped.*
fret, *adorned, preened.*
makis, *mates.*

In this garden, like Palamon and Arcyte seeing Emily, he first sees the Lady—'anon astert/The blude of all my body to my hert'—he describes her rich attire and beauty, begs the nightingale to sing to her, and falls into utter despair at her departure. 'Me thoght the day was turnyt into nyght.' That night he is 'araisit up in-to the aire,/Clippit in a cloude of cristall clere and faire', and transported to Venus' palace. The goddess promises him help, and sends him with Good Hope as guide to Minerva, who teaches him the necessity for truth and virtue in love, and concludes with some remarks on predestination and free-will.

I tuke my leve, als straught as ony lyne,
With-in a beme, that fro the contree dyvine
Sche, percyng throw the firmament, extendit,
To ground ageyne my spirit is descendit.

Quhare, In a lusty plane, tuke I my way,
Endlang a ryver, plesant to behold,
Enbroudin all with freschë flouris gay,
Quhare, throu the gravel, bryght as ony gold,
The cristall water ran so clere and cold,
That In myn erë maid contynualy
A maner soun, mellit with armony;

That full of lytill fishchis by the brym,
Now here, now there, with bakkis blewe as lede,
Lap and playit, and In a rout can swym
So prattily, and dressit tham to sprede
Thaire curall fynnis, as the ruby rede,
That In the sonnë on thaire scalis bryght
As gesserant ay glitterit In my sight.

Enbroudin, *embroidered*.
mellit, *mingled*.
Lap, *leaped*.
curall, *coral*.
gesserant, *burnished armour*.

And by this Ilkë ryver-syde alawe
Ane hyë way thar fand I like to bene
On quhich, on every syde, a longë rawe
Off treis saw I, full of levis grene,
That full of fruyte delitable were to sene,
And also, as It come unto my mynd,
Off bestis sawe I mony diverse kynd:

The lyoun king, and his fere lyonesse;
The pantere, like unto the smaragdyne;
The lytill squerell, full of besynesse;
The slawë asse, the druggare beste of pyne;
The nycë ape, the werely porpapyne;
The percyng lynx, the lufare unicorne,
That voidis venym with his evour horne . . .

Good Hope brings him to Fortune, and he sees her wheel and the
hellish pit beneath it. She bids him climb on to the wheel, and he
awakes.

In the morning, as he is wondering about the dream, a white dove
brings him a branch of flowers, bearing an encouraging message, and
the poem ends in a surfeit of prayers and dedications, commending itself
finally to 'the Impnis (that is, poems) of my maisteris dere, / Gowere and
Chaucere, that on the steppis satt/ Of rethorike, quhill thai were lyvand
here.'

rawe, *row, line.*
fere, *companion.*
smaragdyne, *emerald.*
druggare, *drudging.*
lufare, *lover.*
werely, *warlike.*
voidis, *destroys, repels.*

JAMES IV OF SCOTLAND

Born in 1472. Succeeded to the throne on the assassination of his father, James III, in 1488. Married Margaret Tudor, sister of Henry VIII, and was killed at Flodden in 1513.

Dunbar having petitioned the King for a house to protect him from the winter's cold, speaking in the persona of an old grey horse, the King replied:

After our writings, Treasurer,
Take in this grey horse, Old Dunbar,
Which, in my aucht, with service true
In lyart changèd is in hue;
Gar house him now, against this Yuill,
And busk him like a bishop's mule;
For with my hand I have indost
To pay what ever his trappours cost.

aucht, *possession.*
In lyart, *into grey.*
Yuill, *Christmas.*
busk, *array.*
indost, *endorsed.*
trappours, *housings.*

JAMES V OF SCOTLAND

Born in 1512. Succeeded his father, James IV, on the latter's death at Flodden in 1513. His first wife, Madeleine, daughter of the French King François I, died after only two or three months in Scotland, and James married as his second wife Marie de Guise. He died in 1542, and was succeeded by his six day old daughter, Mary, Queen of Scots.

James is supposed to have written 'Christ's Kirk on the Green', a ballad about a country fair which closely resembles 'Peebles to the Play', and is also attributed to his ancestor James I; I quote verse III:

> Of a' thir maidens, myld as meid,
> Was nane sae jimp as Gillie;
> As ony rose her rude was red,
> Her lyre was lyke the lillie.
> Fow yellow, yellow, was her heid,
> And she of luve sae silly,
> Though a'hir kin had sworn hir deid,
> She wald hae nane but Willie,
> > Alane that day.

jimp, *slender, handsome.*
rude, *blush, face.*
lyre, *flesh.*

There is a great deal more of this, but the other composition attributed to this King, who used to wander about his kingdom disguised, calling himself 'the gudeman of Ballangiech' and joining in his subjects' games and everyday life, seems more worthy of notice—the Ballad of the Gaberlunzie Man (the man who carries a bag on his back, the strolling beggar or tinker). I have modernised some spelling.

> The pauky old carle came o'er the lea
> Wi' many good e'ens and days to me;
> Saying, good wife, for your courtesy,
> > Will ye lodge a silly old man?

> The night was cold, the carle was wat,
> And down ayont the ingle he sat,
> My daughter's shoulders he 'gan to clap,
> > And cadgily ranted and sang.

pauky, *sly, artful.*
wat, *wet.*
ayont the ingle, *beside the hearth.*

O wo! quoth he, were I as free
As first when I saw this countrie,
How blithe and merry would I be,
   And I would ne'er think lang . . .

And O. quoth he, an ye were as black
As e'er the crown of my daddy's hat,
'Tis I would lay thee by my back,
   And away with thee I'd gang.

And O, quoth she, an I were as white
As e'er the snow lay on the dyke,
I'd clothe me braw and ladylike,
   And away with thee I'd gang.

Between the two was made a plot;
They rose a wee before the cock,
And wilily they shot the lock,
   And fast to the bent they are gane.

Upon the morn the old wife raise
And at her leisure put on her claise;
Syne to the servant's bed she gaes,
   To speer for the silly poor man.

She gaed to the bed where the beggar lay,
The straw was cold, he was away,
She clapt her hands, cried, dulefuday,
   For some of our gear will be gone!

. . . The servant gaed where the daughter lay,
The sheets were cold, she was away;
And fast to her goodwife 'gan say,
   She's off with the gaberlunzie man.

a wee, *a little while.*
bent, *downs.*
speer, *look.*

O fy gar ride, and fy gar rin,
And haste ye find these traitors again;
For she'll be burnt, and he'll be slain,
   The wearisome gaberlunzie man.

Some rode upon horse, some ran a-fit,
The wife was wude, and out o' her wit;
She could na gang, nor yet could she sit,
   But aye she cursed and she banned.

Mean time far hind out o'er the lea,
Fu' snug in a glen where none could see,
The two with kindly sport and glee
   Cut from a new cheese a whang;

The priving was good, it pleased them both,
To love her for ay he gave her his oath;
Quoth she, to leave thee I will be loath,
   My winsome gaberlunzie man.

. . . My dear, quoth he, ye're yet o'er young,
And have not learned the beggar's tongue,
To follow me from town to town,
   And carry the gaberlunzie on.

With cauk and keel I'll win your breed,
And spindles and whorls for them who need,
Which is a gentle trade indeed,
   To carry the gaberlunzie on.

I'll bow my leg, and crook my knee,
And draw a black clout o'er my eye,
A cripple, or blind, will they call me,
   While we shall be merry and sing.

wude, *mad.*
banned, *cursed, raved.*
whang, *long thin slice.*
priving, *first taste.*
cauk and keel, *charlatan's fortune-telling tricks*(?).
breed, *bread, food.*

72

MARY QUEEN OF SCOTS

Mary Stuart. Born in 1542, Daughter of James V. Married Francis II of France and later Lord Darnley, and later still Bothwell. She was apprehended and imprisoned by Elizabeth I and finally beheaded on a charge of conspiring against Elizabeth's life in 1587.

Verses on the death of her first husband, François II, King of France, 1560.

En mon triste et doux chant,
D'un ton fort lamentable,
Je jette un oeil tranchant
De perte incomparable,
Et en soupirs cuisans
Passe mes meilleurs ans.

Fut-il un tel malheur,
De dure destinée,
Ni si triste douleur
De dame fortunée
Qui mon coeur et mon oeil
Vois en bierre et cercueil?

Qui en mon doux printemps
Et fleur de ma jeunesse
Toutes les peines sens
D'une extrême tristesse,
Et en rien n'ay plaisir,
Qu'en regret et desir.

Ce qui m'estoit plaisant
Ores m'est peine dure;
Le jour le plus luisant
M'est nuit noire et obscure,
Et n'est rien si exquis
Qui de moy soit requis.

In my sad sweet song of mournful tune, I cast a piercing glance upon my incomparable loss, and spend my best years in painful sighs. Was there ever such a disaster brought by harsh destiny, nor such sad grief endured by a fortunate lady? I see my heart and my eyes on the bier and in the coffin. In my sweet spring and the flower of my youth I feel all the pains of extreme sadness, and take pleasure in nothing but mourning and longing. What used to be pleasant to me is now harsh pain; the brightest day is dull dark night, and there is nothing so exquisite that I desire it.

J'ay au coeur et à l'oeil
Un portrait et image
Qui figure mon dueil
Et mon pasle visage,
De violettes teint,
Qui est l'amoureux teint.

Pour mon mal estranger
Je ne m'arreste en place;
Mais j'en ay eu beau changer,
Si ma douleur j'efface.
Car mon pis et mon mieux
Sont mes plus deserts lieux.

Si en quelque sejour,
Soit en bois ou en prée,
Soit pour l'aube du jour,
Ou soit pour la vesprée,
Sans cesse mon coeur sent
Le regret d'un absent.

Si par fois vers ces lieux
Viens à dresser ma veuë,
Le doux trait de ses yeux
Je vois en une nuë.
Soudain je vois en l'eau
Comme dans un tombeau.

Within my heart and eye is a pictured image that shows forth my mourning and my violet-pale face—the colour of lovers. In order to escape my unhappiness, I move about from place to place, but I have changed in vain, if I efface my grief. For me the worst and the best are the most solitary places. If I am resting in meadow or wood, at dawn or evening, constantly my heart longs for one who is absent. If sometimes I glance towards those places, I see the gentle light of his looks in a cloud. I see him in the water as though in a tomb.

Si je suis en repos,
Sommeillant sur ma couche,
J'oy qu'il me tient propos,
Je le sens qu'il me touche,
En labeur, en recoy,
Tousjours est pres de moy.

Je ne vois autre objet,
Pour beau qu'il se presente;
A qui que soit subjet
Onques mon coeur consente,
Exempt de perfection
A cette affection.

Mets, Chanson, icy fin
A si triste complainte,
Dont sera le refrein
Amour vraye et non feinte;
Pour la separation
N'aura diminution.

If I am resting, dozing on my bed, I hear him talking to me, I feel him touch me; at work or at rest, he is always near me. I see nothing else, however fine it appears; my heart agrees to no other subject; all are lacking in perfection when compared with this. Here end, my song, your sad lament, whose refrain will be true and unfeigned love; separation will not lessen it.

Ung seul penser qui me profficte et nuit
Amer et doulx change en mon coeur sans cesse;
Entre le doubte et l'espoir il m'oppresse
Tant que la paix et la repos me fuit.

Donc, chere soeur, si ceste carte suit
L'affection de vous veoir qui me presse,
C'est que je viz en peine et en tristesse
Si promtement l'effect ne s'en ensuit.

J'ay veu la nef relascher par contraincte
En haulte mer, proche d'entrer au port,
Et le serain se convertir en trouble.

Ainsi je suis en soucy et en crainte
Non pas de vous, mais quantes fois à tort
Fortune rompt voille et cordage double.

One thought alone that brings me harm and good mingles bitter and sweet in my heart without end, oppresses me until peace and rest flee from me, keeps me between doubt and hope. So, dear sister, if this paper expresses the insistent wish I have to see you, it is because I live in torment and sadness, if quickly it does not bring the (wished-for) result.

I have seen a ship go out of control on the high seas, just before entering harbour, and clear weather turn foul. Thus I remain in fear and anxiety, not for you—but sometimes Fortune cruelly breaks our sails and (even) double rigging.

Poem to the Bishop of Ross on his release from prison, 1574

Puisque Dieu a, par sa bonté imence,
Permis qu'ayez obtins tant de bon heur,
De despartir en credit et faveur
Hors de prison, en sayne conscience,

Remerciez sa divine clemence,
Qui de tous biens est seul cause et autheur,
Et le priez d'un humble et devot coeur
Qu'il ayt pitie de ma longue souffrance.

Since through his immeasurable goodness God has permitted you such good fortune as to depart from prison with a clear conscience and a restored reputation, give thanks to his divine clemency, he who is sole cause and author of all good things, and pray him with humble and devout heart to have pity on my long sufferings. (Mary herself had been in prison in England since 1568.)

Poem from Bodleian MS. Arch.F.c.8

Que suis-je, helas, et de quoy sert ma vie.
Je'n suis fors q'un corps privé de cueur
Un ombre vayn, un object de malheur,
Qui n'a plus rien que de mourir envie.
Plus ne portez, o enemis! d'envie
À qui n'a plus l'esprit à la grandeur,
Ja consommé d'exsessive doulleur:
Vottre ire en brief ce voirra assovie.
Et vous, amys! qui m'avez tenu chere,
Souvenez vous que sans heur, sans santy,
Je ne scaurois aucun bon oeuvre fayre.
Souhaitez donc fin de calamitay.
Et que, sa bas estant asses punie,
J'aye ma part en la joye infinie.

What am I, alas, and what use is my life? I am nothing but a body without a heart, a vain shadow, an object of misfortune, that wants nothing but to die. Oh my enemies, envy no longer one whose spirit is no longer suited to grandeur, but is consumed by its overwhelming grief; soon your fury will be satisfied. And you, my friends who have held me dear, think that I could accomplish no good work, being thus without health or fortune; wish, then, for an end to my misery, and that, having been sufficiently punished here on earth, I may share in the infinite joy of heaven.

Said to have been composed on the morning of her execution, February 8th, 1578:

O Domine Deus, speravi in te.
O care me Jesu, nunc libera me
In dura catena, in misera poena, desidero
Languendo, gemendo, et genu flectendo
Adoro, imploro ut liberes me.

    O Lord God, I have hoped in Thee. O Jesus dear to me, free me now; in hard chains and wretched suffering, I desire, languishing, groaning and bending the knee, I adore Thee, implore Thee to free me.

HENRY STEWART, LORD DARNLEY

Born in 1546. Son of Lady Margaret Douglas, half-sister of James V of Scotland. In 1565, married his step-first cousin, Mary Queen of Scots, and was created Duke of Albany and King Consort. As a descendant of Henry VII, he had like Mary herself a claim to the English throne, although a foreigner and a Catholic. In 1566 his son James VI and I was born, and in the following year Darnley perished in the explosion at Kirk o'Field, murdered by a gang of conspirators that included Bothwell, later the Queen's third husband.

Poem to the Queen, from the Bannatyne MS.

Gife langour makis men light
Or dolour thame decoir
In erth thair is no wight
May me compare in gloir;
Gif cairful thoftes restoir
My havy hairt from sorrow,
I am for evir moir
In joy both evin and morrow.

Gif pleser be to pance
I playnt me nocht opprest,
Or absence micht advance,
My hairt is haill possest;
Gif want of quiet rest
From cairis might me convoy,
My mind is nocht mollest,
Bot evir moir in joy.

Gif, gife, *if.*
thame decoir, *adorns them.*
thoftes, *thoughts.*
pance, *think, dream.*
haill, *wholly.*
mollest, *vexed.*

Thought that I pance in paine,
In passing to and fro,
I labour all in vaine,
For so hes many mo,
That hes not servit so,
In suiting of their sueit.
The nare the fyre I go,
The grittar is my heat.

The turtour for her maik
Mair dule may not indure,
Nor I do for hir saik,
Evin her quha hes in cure
My hairt, quhilk sal be sure
And service to the deid,
Unto that lady pure
The well of womanheid.

Schaw, schedull, to that sueit
My pairt so permanent
That no mirth quhill we meit
Sall cause me be content;
Bot still my hairt lament
In sorrowfull siching soir,
Till tyme scho be present.
Fairweill, I say no moir.

ffinis q king hary stewart

sueit, *beloved*.
nare, *closer to*.
grittar, *greater*.
turtour, *turtle-dove*.
maik, *mate*.
Nor, *than*.
to the deid, *until my death*.
schedull, *little paper*.
quhill, *until*.

Advice to a Prince, by 'henrye stewart', also from the Bannatyne MS.

Be governor baith guid and gratious
Be leill and luifand to thy liegis all
Be large of fredome and no thing desyrous
Be just to pure for ony thing may fall
Be ferme of faith and constant as ane wall
Be reddye evir to stanche evill and discord
Be cheretabill and sickerlye thow sall
Be bowsum ay to knaw thy god and lord

Be nocht to proud of wardlie guidis heir
Be weill be-thocht thai will remane na tyde
Be sicker als that thow man die but weir
Be war thairwith the tyme will no man byde
Be vertewus and sett all vyce on syde
Be patient lawlie and misericord
Be rewlit so quhair evir thow go or byde
Be bowsum ay to knaw thy god and lord

Be weill avysit of quhome thow counsale tais
Be sever of thame that thai be leill and trew
Be-think the als quhidder thai be freindis or fais
Be to thy saull thair sawis or thow persew
Be nevir o'er haistye to wirk and syne to rew
Be nocht thair freind/ that makis the fals record
Be reddye evir all guid works to renew
Be bowsum ay to knaw thy god and Lord

luifand, *loving.*
for ony thing may fall, *whatever happens.*
sickerlye, *surely.*
bowsum, *obedient.*
wardlie guidis, *worldly goods.*
but weir, *without doubt.*
byde, *wait for.*
lawlie and misericord, *humble and merciful.*
quhidder, *whether.*
sawis, *advice, maxims.*
syne, *afterwards.*

Be traist and conquese thy awin heretage
Be ennemyes of auld now occupyit
Be strenth and force thow sobir thai man swage
Be law of god/ thair may no man denyid
Be nocht as Lantern in mirknes unspyit
Be thow in rycht thi Landis suld be restord
Be wirschop so thy name beis magnefeit
Be bowsum ay to knaw thy god and Lord

Be to rebellis strong as lyoun eik
Be ferce to follow thame quhair evir thai found
Be to thy Liege men bayth soft and meik
Be thair succor and help thame haill and sound
Be knaw thy cure and caus quhy thow was cround
Be besye evir/ that justice be nocht smord
Be blyith in hart thir wordis oft expound
Be bowsum ay to knaw thy god and Lord

Be traist and conquese, *by treachery and conquest.*
'thou sobir thai man swage' is not clear; I tentatively suggest *'you must with moderation appease them'.*
in mirknes unspyit, *unseen in darkness.*
wirschop, *honour.*
Be knaw thy cure, *be aware of thy office and purpose as ruler.*
smord, *smothered, extinguished.*

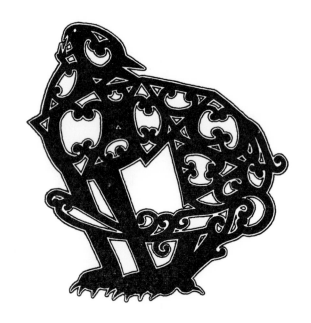

HYWEL AB OWAIN GWYNEDD

Hywel ab Owain Gwynedd. Son of Owain ab Gruffyd ab Cynan,
prince of North Wales, by the daughter of an Irish nobleman. Lived a
fiercely battling life, fighting his brothers, his uncle, the invading
Normans, and Gruffyd ab Rhys, prince of South Wales, and is said to
have died in Ireland in 1170. Eight of his poems are still extant.

In summer

I love summer-time, stallions' trampling,
Men high-hearted before a brave lord;
Foaming the wave, swiftly coursing;
Apple-tree gowned, one more token;
Blazing my buckler, shouldered for battle.
I craved what I lacked, despite longing—
Tall white hemlock, gently bending,
The hue of fair dawn at mid-day,
Frail bright form, smooth, white, and pliant.
As she walks, barely bent is the rush,
Little darling, light is her footstep.
Scarcely older than a girl of ten,
Child-like, well-formed, full of comeliness.
Young she was trained to be bountiful;
Young woman, more passion will come to the fair
Than unseemly speech from her lips.
Pacing, pleading, shall I have a tryst?
How long must I ask you? Come meet me.
Without measure my vows in love's madness:
Jesus will spare me, he understands.

My Choice

My chosen, a maid fair and slender,
Tall and white, in her heather-hued gown.
And my chosen lore, to watch one who's womanly,
When she speaks, scarcely heard, gracious words.
And my chosen part, to contend with a girl,
Private together, for gift, for grace.
This I have chosen, wave's lovely shade,
Seer of your shire, your pure Welsh speech.
My chosen you are: what am I to you?
Why be still (lovely your silence)?
I've chosen a girl, one I'll never regret;
Rightly is chosen so fair a choice.

Celebration

A foaming white wave washes a grave,
Rhufawn Befr's tomb, ruler of monarchs.

88

I love, England's bane, the bright Northland today,
    And the flourishing groves by the Lliw.
    I love the place that sates me with mead,
    Where the seas come in, ceaseless turmoil.
I love its band of men and its stout homesteads,
    At its ruler's wish stirring up strife.
    I love its sea-coast and its mountains
    And its wood-bordered fort and fine lands,
    And its watered dells and its valleys,
    And its white gulls and comely women.
    I love its soldiers and its trained steeds
    And its woods and strong men and dwellings.
I love its meadows and its small rich clover
    Where fame had a firm joyful welcome.
    I love its lowlands, bravery's due,
    And its wide wilderness and its wealth.
    Ah sole Son of God, great the wonder,
    Such fine war-stags, so sturdily framed.
    I did superb work with a spear-thrust
    Between Powys' force and fair Gwynedd.
    And on a white steed, surfeit of strife,
    May I win a release from exile.
I will not endure till my war-band comes,
    A dream says this and God decrees it.
    A foaming white wave washes a grave.

    A foaming white wave, bold by homesteads,
    Hue of hoar-frost as it is cresting.
    I love the sea-strand of Meiroinydd
    Where I had a white arm for pillow.
    I love the nightingale in privet
    Where two rivers meet, valley of praise.
    Lord of heaven and earth, Gwynedd's king,
    How far from Ceri, Caer Lliwelydd!
    I rode a bay mount from Maelienydd
    Far as Rheged, by night and by day.
    May I win before death a new prize,
    In Tegeingl, the fairest in the land.
    Though a lover in Ovid's fashion,
    God be mindful of me when dying.
    A foaming white wave, bold by homesteads.

OWAIN CYFEILIOG

Owain Cyfeiliog. Prince of Powys, son of Gruffyd ab Maredudd. Known for his wise rule, generous hospitality, and ready wit. Fought with Owain Gwynedd and Rhys of South Wales against the Normans. Became a Cistercian at the abbey of Strata Marcella, which he had founded, and died there in 1197.

The drinking-horn

As dawn arose, battle was joined,
Enemies hurling a worthless threat.
Red-speared our men, after heavy labour,
Maelor's fortress wall saw havoc.
Nobles I sent to the struggle,
Fearless in combat, red-weaponed.
Who vexes a hero had best beware:
Wrath's expected once he is roused.
Cup-bearer, what stills me, may it stay mine,
Bring the horn for drinking together,
Full of yearning, tinted, ninth wave's hue,
Long and blue its designs, gold its trim.
Fill to the brim, cup-bearer, with joy
The horn in Rhys' hand at a rich court,
Owain's court, a king's, forever feasting,
Haven of suppliants, doors unbarred,
And bear the long-pledged drink of bragget
To Gwgawn's hand because of his deed:
Cubs of Goronwy, savage fury's assault,
Cubs quick of foot, courageous their deed,
Men who merit reward when hard-pressed,
Men of worth in war, sturdy defence,
Shepherds of Hafren, proud when they hear
The din of mead-horns, plenty in store.

Fill the horn brim-full for Cynfelyn,
Redoubted, made drunk by foaming mead,
And if you would live another year
Pay him full respect, as is proper.
And bring to Gruffudd, red-speared foeman.
Wine in a bright crystal container,
War-lord of Arwystli, border's trust,
War-lord of kind Owain, Cynfyn's heir,
War-lord who stirs, is not stricken by, strife,
Carnage in clash, peril in pursuit.
Warriors went for the praise of glory,
Companions in arms, armed savagely.
They earned their mead, as Belyn's men once did:
Well may they drink while any man lives.

Fill the horn to the brim, for I propose
   To drink with a lord whose talk sparkles,
   In Ednyfein's hand, war's commander,
   Lightning under a broad light buckler,
In Ednyfedd's hand, heroic lion,
   Brave thrust of spear, shaven thin his shield.
   Firm in turmoil, both free of fear,
   They slash, slicing wind above fair land,
   Furrows in the ranks in battle's brunt.
   A gold-chased shield-face they swiftly slash,
   Deep-dyed are their spears after piercing,
   Skilful attacking a splendid camp.
   I heard in Maelor a sudden roar,
   A harsh cry of men and sharp fury,
   And convening round wine-cups they prowl,
   As once in Bangor round an ash fire
   When two monarchs fought above mead-horns
   At the revels of Morach Morfran.

Fill the horn to the brim, for I ponder
   How they fought for mead and our kingdom,
   Fearless Selyf, safeguard of Gwygyr,
   Let him cringe who irks him, eagle's heart,
And Madawg's sole son, renowned Tudur Hael,
   True warrior, hewer, lightning with lance,
   Two heroes, two lions in combat,
   Two fierce forces, two sons of Ynyr,
   Two free, that day, in giving fight,
   Twin arches, unyielding, peerless deed,
   Lions' lashing at thrusting soldiers,
   Lords of war, marauders, red their spears,
   Firm pressure of terror, rapid rout,
   Shorn their two shields, with a single aim:
   The shouting wind shattered the sea-bank,
   Sudden force of famous Talgarth's waves.

Fill brim-full, cup-bearer, court not death,
   The horn much-honoured in revels,
   Long blue drinking-horn, revered of old,
   Silver-embossed, not narrow-lipped,
   And bring to Tudur, armies' eagle,
   The ritual drink of dark red wine.

Unless there's fetched of first-class mead
A goblet of drink, off goes your head,
For Moreiddig's hand, sponsor of songs,
Forebears' praise before cold burial.
Marvellous brothers, both high-minded,
Unequalled power beneath their brows,
Soldiers who gave to me good service,
Not stained, stainless, not faulty, faultless,
Warfarers, routers, war-leaders, wolves,
Savage ferocity, bloodstained spears.
Proud is Mochnannwys' lord in Powys
Hearing of how the two of them fought.
Saviours when needed, red their weapons,
They held their borders against a host.
Praise is their portion, these I speak of—
Keening has come, both taken from me:
Ah Christ! how grieved am I by the pain
Of Moreiddig's loss, much is he missed.

Fill the horn, since they ask it of me,
Long, blue, merrily for Morbant's hand,
Man who deserves a song, special praise,
Bitter his blade, deep-piercing spear-thrust,
A man of great worth, suffering much,
Sword smooth on both sides, keen its edges.
Fill, cup-bearer, from silver service
A gift of glory with reverence:
At Gwestwn Fawr I saw a marvel,
Goronwy's stand was a hundred's deed.
Warriors, one in purpose, performed it,
Bearers of battle, careless of life:
A lord and his enemies met in war,
A steward was slain, a sea-fort burned,
A precious prisoner they brought forth.
Each man was sweating when they returned,
Filled with sun were high hill and valley.

Fill the horn brim-full for the warriors,
Owain's cubs, brave men striking as one,
Worthy ones, in a place of honour,
Constant where they go the bright blades' strokes,
Madawg and Meilyr, men accustomed

94

To conflict, against iniquity,
Battle's thunderers, wise in warfare,
Strife-sowing men, sturdy defenders.
I have heard for mead men went to Catraeth,
Proper their purpose, weapons deep-dyed.
Mynyddawg's troops, for their sleep in death,
Had the tale that's told, hate-stirred war-lords.
No worse did my warriors in Maelor's strife,
Freeing a prisoner, deed worth praise.

Fill brim-full, cup-bearer, with clear sweet mead,
Battle of spear-blows, sweat under stress,
From horns the splendid golden-rimmed horn
For fame earned in return for their lives.
Of the sleepless pain sustained by lords
None knows but God and he that speaks it.
One who swears not, pays not, plays not false,
Daniel, loyal war-lord, how rare and true.
Cup-bearer, how many times are spared
Men death will not spare, till they grow spoiled.
Cup-bearer, the mead-feast I share,
Strong fire bright-gleaming, torches' strong glow.
Cup-bearer, you saw rage in Llidwm:
Men I honour, they will be honoured.
Cup-bearer, you saw the armour of lords
Encircling Owain, a savage shield.
When Cawres fell, hot fighting needed,
The ruinous plunder will be praised.
Cup-bearer, leave not, I'll not be left:
May we be received in Paradise
By the Lord of kings, long be our welcome,
In the place one sees true protection.